CONTENTS

140 Years of US – Romanian Relations

Partners without a Partnership

ALEXANDRU CRISTIAN

FOREWORD – PARTNERS WITHOUT A PARTNERSHIP

Romania and the United States of America share some history which is similar in many respects. Both states have struggled to gain their independence, their sovereignty, and historical recognition. That in which they have followed a different path was pertaining to the civilization pattern in which each of the two states was established.

We need to remind here, and pay all the due respect to them, the Romanian and American historians who have dealt with the early issues of the US-Romanian relations, that is Paul Cernovodeanu, Cornelia Bodea, Ion Stanciu, Dumitru Vitcu, Constantin Buşe, Keith Hitchins, Stephen Fischer-Galaţi, Radu R. Florescu, James F. Clarke, and many others.

The US-Romanian relations celebrate 140 years of an extremely challenging existence, which has eventually proved both states' admiration for the civilization pattern – Romania for acquiring its national independence and for implementing a genuine democratic model, whereas the United States of America for the cultural and linguistic miracle represented by the Romanian people. There has been a joint history which proved to both peoples what a struggle for being acknowledged by history meant.

The history of the United States of America has been written with outstanding sacrifice just like the one of our country, while both countries have suffered for being overridden. In the very year 1764, before gaining its independence, on *July 4th, 1776*, a pamphlet signed by Isaac Hunt was published, which compared the state of colonized America to the one in Transylvania, and in which the governor of the British crown was compared to the Transylvanian vaivode. That is quite a suggestive piece of writing about the value of the peoples' freedom. After having become independent, the United States of America would launch into a continental and commercial territorial expansion rarely seen in the history of mankind. Guided by that ***Manifest Destiny***, the American people has continued to enlarge the soil on which the American nation and consciousness have been shaped, by the end of the 19th century the new state was to become a true competitor of the hegemonic of that time, the British Empire, only to outperform the latter.

The tumultuous 19th century brought for our country the unification of the two Romanian principalities, the reign of a foreign ruler, the turning of our country into a kingdom, and the continuous modernizing of the new Romanian state. Tudor Vladimirescu's 1821 uprising, the 1848 Revolution, the 1859 Unification, and the proclamation of the independence, followed by the Independence War are all historic landmarks having helped turn the Romanian countries into a new modern state.

The official diplomatic relations between Romania and the United States of America were established on June 11, 1880, by having the first US diplomatic representative to our country appointed. Prior to establishing those relations, there have been intensive diplomatic and commercial contacts between our country and the United States of America.

This study is dedicated to the Romanian-American relations since their very beginning until the Great Unification. We have analysed the factors which have drawn closer the two countries separated by a large distance, the precise distance between the two capital-cities, Bucharest and Washington D.C. being 7,977.6 kilometres. We need to add that this study is the early stage of some broader and more complex research.

1 PRELIMINARIES OF THE US-ROMANIAN RELATIONS

Communication between the two states could only be possible due to the technological and scientific evolution of mankind. The two industrial revolutions allowed these two states to get closer to each other. Let's not forget the commercial spread of the young North-American state. The invention of the steam engine and the use thereof on large ships have connected the Old and the New World, and thus the relations have developed between the Romanian Principalities and the United States of North America, as they used to be called in the press and in the studies of the time drafted in the Romanian countries.

The first factor to help establish such relations was the commercial importance of the Danubian principalities at the entrance of the Danube, as the Romanian countries used to have harbours to the Black Sea. **The second factor** was the willingness of the United States of America to conclude commercial treaties and to establish commercial routes to enable them to develop their trade, as economy has always relied on active trade. **The third factor** was cultural, namely the scientific competition of the Enlightenment century, as well as the emergence of the worldwide modernization by means of the new technological conquests.

The first accounts on the Romanian countries are to be found with the explorer John Smith, who described the events following Michael the Brave's assassination in 1601, and the destruction of the unification hopes of the three Romanian territories in his travel memoirs. John Smith (1580-1631) arrived to America in 1605 and he explored the continent until 1609. He was the one to borrow his name to the region in the North-Eastern part of the American state which currently comprises the states of Maine, Vermont, New Hampshire, Massachusetts, Rhode Island, and Connecticut, connecting that area to New England, a region currently sharing the border with the state of New York and the present-day Canada.

The first inhabitant of the Romanian principalities certified on the American soil was the Saxon reverend Johannes Kelp, who settled in Pennsylvania at the end of the 17th century to preach puritanism.

An interesting moment related to the first Romanian-American contacts is the one when one of the founding fathers of the United States, the scientist Benjamin Franklin (1706-1790) and the Transylvanian Orthodox priest Samuilă Damian got into contact as they were both very fond of science. Father Damian is a pioneer of the study of electricity in our country. As he travelled from England to America, he met Franklin in 1748, an encounter that the great scientist described in his memoirs. Samuilă Damian then travelled to Jamaica, to the New Spain – the current Mexico, and nothing has been reported about him since then. Worried, Franklin wrote in his memoirs that the priest might have died on the road.

We mentioned Hunt's pamphlet above. We should also add that there has been a colony called *Transylvania* in the state of Kentucky between 1775 and 1777.

John Quincy Adams (1767-1848), US ambassador to Petersburg in the Russian Empire from 1809 until 1814[1], mentioned the situation of the Romanian countries in his information to the Department of State – notes sent to the secretary of state James Monroe[2].

The American ambassador informed James Monroe about the intention to initiate relations with the Danubian principalities, and to get closer to the South-Eastern part of Europe. John Quincy Adams then served as the US Secretary of State from 1817 until 1825, and as a President of the United States of America between 1825 and 1829. His mission was to be pursued by the following American ambassador to Petersburg, Henry Middleton, in office from 1820 until 1830. In his information reports sent to the Department of State, the latter mentioned the fight of Alexandru Ipsilanti's (1792-1828) *Filiki Eteria*, Tudor Vladimirescu's (around 1780-1821) 1821 uprising, the

---

[1] The designation of the time was minister plenipotentiary of the United States to Russia.

[2] James Monroe (1758-1831), Secretary of State of the United States of America between 1811-1817, *President of the United States of America* between 1817-1825, creator of the famous Monroe Doctrine, announced on December 2nd, 1823, which ruled that the European powers would not interfere in the newly established states in North and South America anymore, nor would they colonize that part of the world anymore.

struggle for independence of Greece, and the sacrifice mission of the famous English poet Lord George Gordon Byron (1788- 1824).

The first extensive historical description of the Romanian Principalities was published in October 1828 in Boston in *The North American Review*: a historical study reflecting a thorough knowledge of the domestic situation of the Romanian Principalities. A historic journey which also made reference to the matter of tribute (taxes) paid since Mircea the Old's reign (he lived around 1355- 1418, and ruled between 1386-1418).

The American Department of State sent important orders to its diplomatic agents in Constantinople on September 12, 1829. Those orders included the incentives of the American president James Buchanan (1791-1868, serving as a president from 1857 until 1861) to initiate new commercial routes to connect the Bosporus Strait and the Black Sea; the first commercial treaty between the United States of America and the Ottoman Empire thus came into force on May 10, 1831, a fact which has brought the US closer to the Danubian Principalities.

The American consul in Constantinople, John Brown urged in 1839 the Department of Stat to establish consular offices with a vice-consular rank in the Romanian harbours at the Danube, following the English model[3]. Along with this urge, he enclosed the report of Charles Cunnigham, vice-consul, then consul of England to Galați and Brăila from 1836 until 1860, on the trade in the Romanian harbours

---

[3] The American ambassador was David Porter, a very good American diplomat.

at the Danube, a report drafted on December 31st, 1838. With this report, the consul also sent information needed to make a decision. According to historians Paul Cernovodeanu and Ion Stanciu, this is the very *first informative material received by the Department of State of the United States of America about our country.*

Pursuant to the reports of the Austrian consul to Iași, a certain John Bradish was appointed consul of the United States to Galați in 1844, yet the Department of State has never endorsed him. The first commercial vessel under American flag, **Acafi**, arrived to Brăila on October 10, 1843, this event marking the first direct contact between the two states. According to other sources, the first American ship got to the Sulina horn or to the Galați harbour in 1844. *The inconsistency of such data is not relevant, what matters is that the United States of America have developed a commercial route with the Romanian countries less than seven decades after they were established as a state.*

In 1850, *Gazeta de Moldova* and *Journal de Bucharest* announced that the industrialist Anton Negroponte was appointed vice-consul of the United States of America to Galați, a honorary position subordinated to the American office in Constantinople, and to the American ambassador George Perkins Marsh, the one who preceded in office Caroll Spence, to be mentioned below. The consular office has lasted for three years. It was suspended by the American President Franklin Pierce (1804-1869, in office from 1853 until 1857). The activity of the vice-consulates in Brussa and Dardanelles was suspended along the office in Galați. Yet the Galați-born entrepreneur Anton Negroponte struggles to have this consular office preserved; his insistence made it be reopened in

1857.

The narratives on the Romanian states become more and more numerous, an increasing number of observers take an interest in the evolution of the small Danubian states.

An interesting account on life back during that time in the Romanian states is due to James Oscar Noyes, an American surgeon serving in the Ottoman army during the War of Crimea (1853-1856), and a correspondent of *The New York Daily Tribune*.

The American diplomat Caroll Spence (1818-1896), the American ambassador to Constantinople between 1853 and 1857 was a fierce supporter of the matter of the Romanian Principalities. *Spence has always stated the Principalities' right to get united and become autonomous.*

On March 16, 1858 the American President James Buchanan (1791-1868, in office between 1857 and 1861) sent to the American Senate the nomination of the first American career consul to Galați (Moldova) as Henry T. Romertze. The consul received the position acknowledgement from the Ottomans on April 4, and the acceptance of the ruler Alexandru Ioan Cuza in October. The Romanian ruler emphasized that the American government had to first address the Romanian government, and subsequently the Ottoman one. The consul submitted his letters of acknowledgement on November 10, 1859 in the military camp of Florești. Alexandru Ioan Cuza passed the message to Romertze that he accepted his nomination as a sign of respect for the American government and people, and that he required that all the institutions in both principalities acknowledge the latter as a United States consul. Moreover, Cuza proposed a cooperation, trade, and navigation treaty, yet the American government declined his offer as it feared negative response from the Ottomans. Such a treaty was to come into force after our country acquired its independence.

1.1 DIPLOMATIC RELATIONS PRIOR TO INSTITUTIONALIZATION

We must emphasize that the United States of America wished to enhance its relations with the United Principalities, but the suzerainty of the Ottoman Empire and the potential consequences on the Black Sea trade made the American governments wait for the appropriate time to improve the diplomatic, economic, and cultural relations. After the vice-consulate in Galați was established, some other American consulates were created, one to Ismail in 1860, one to Brăila in 1861, and one to Iași in 1861; those consulates have not been operating for long, nor did they have much business because the first consulate general of the United States was set to Bucharest.

The first consulate general of the United States of America to Bucharest was established in 1864, the first consul being Adolf Hartman, who had been a consul to Galați. After Hartman's short term, Louis Czapkay, of Hungarian origin, but residing in California was appointed consul on June 20, 1866. The new consul proposed the vice-consulate in Galați be directly subordinated to the one in Bucharest instead of the American legation in Constantinople. Czapkay was a consul committed to enhancing the Romanian-American relations, and for these reasons he drafted reports on the political, social, and economic situation of the new Romanian state.

During this period, we need to emphasize the mission of Major Nicoale Dabija, the representative of the ruler Carol I (1839-1914, prince from 1866 until 1881, and king from 1881 until 1914) for concluding collaboration contracts and agreements with the American weapon manufacturing firms. The Romanian army had been equipped with 25,000 Peabody rifles and with steam machinery able to manufacture 3,000 metal bullets a day prior to Major Dabija's mission to Prussia. In December 1868, Major Dabija announced the prince that the mission was successfully completed, and that the army could be equipped for acquiring the country's independence.

An interesting character was the consul succeeding to Czapkay, Benjamin F. Peixotto (1834-1890), in office from 1870 until 1875: a consul struggling to have the difficult Jewish matter settled. His mission resulted in the action he took to make the stakeholders aware of the settlement of that issue.

The American consul to Galați, Alexander C. Hepites, in office between 1872 and 1878, was a tireless diplomat who sent many informative reports on the American citizens living or working in the Danubian harbours. The American consul drafted reports about the Romanian harbours based on the trade documents regarding the export and import operations issued by the latter; we can thus notice those Romanian river gates towards the Black Sea were quite busy. Consul Hepites supported the need to galvanize the trade between the two states and he proposed to create a direct commercial trade to connect New York and the Galați and Brăila harbours.

In 1874, the minister of foreign affairs Vasile Boerescu (1830 – 1883) endorsed the arrival of an American committee made of officers and engineers specialized in hydrography to perform studies on the Danube hydrographic basin and to support performing works at the Danube horns.

The United States of America were interested in our country's fate and the backed the latter's efforts to acquire its independence. Following the 1877-1878 War of Independence, the American government acknowledged Romania's independence. On May 23rd, 1878 the Galați consul Timothy Smith arrived to Bucharest and Bucharest and handed to the Romanian authorities a letter from the US President Rutherford Birchard Hayes (1822-1893, in office from 1877 until 1881), a handwritten letter in which the US president acknowledged the independence and sovereignty of Romania. On October 15, 1878 that letter was also published in New York Times. When submitting his endorsement letters, consul Smith passed to the prince Charles the Ith the full acknowledgement of the independence, telling him that the Romanian-American relations would be enhanced and would evolve towards institutionalization and a permanent status.

Soon, just as he had promised, the American president endorsed the American government to institutionalize the Romanian-American relations. The Secretary of State of the United States of America William Maxwell Evarts (1818-1901, in office from 1877 until 1881) thus signed the document accrediting to Bucharest the first diplomatic agent and consul general of the United States of America close to the government of His Royal Highness, a document signed on June 11, 1880. The same paper appointed Eugene Schuyler as diplomatic agent and consul general of the United States of America to Romania with his residence in Bucharest.

2 MAKING THE US-ROMANIAN RELATIONS OFFICIAL AND PERMANENT

Another important moment in the Romanian-American relations occurren in the same year 1880. That was Colonel Sergiu Voinescu's mission in the United States of America, the representative of the prince Charles the I[st]. The mission assigned was to notify the American government about the new international status of our country, namely that it has acquired its independence and sovereignty as a state.

With the help of Eugene Schuyler, a diplomat who had must supported out country, colonel Voinescu got plenty of recommendations which made his entry to the deputy of the Secretary of State John Hay (1838-1905)[4] easier. John Hay shall become a

---

[4] During the period 1853-1913, the deputy of the Secretary of State was appointed Assistant Secretary of State. According to the department hierarchy, the position as an assistant was practically the one of a substitute for the Secretary of State at

Secretary of State of the United States from 1898 until 1905. Colonel Voinescu was very well received due to the recommendations from Schuyler and he accomplished his mission successfully. He was received by the US President Rutherford Birchard Hayes, who emphasized that the economic relations between the two countries need to get enhanced for the benefit of both countries. Moreover, the president of the United States of America told colonel Voinescu that enhancing the relations also involved sending a permanent representative f our country to Washington D.C., a fact approved by colonel Voinescu, who added that the budgetary resources did not allow for the time being to establish a Romanian office in the United States.

The American president handed to colonel Voinescu a letter to Charles the Ist, dated November 20, 1880, a letter making his collaboration and friendship relations between the two states clear.

At the colonel Voinescu's request and with John Hay's help, the Secretary of State of the United States William Maxwell Evarts sent him a special recommendation for the American military authorities, thus having some American military bases authorized by colonel Voinescu, more precisely at Hartford – Connecticut, and others. The mission is successfully completed, while colonel Voinescu heartily thanked John Hay and all the American friends, only to get back to Romania in February 1881.

---

the management of the Department of State. This position is currently called *Deputy Secretary of State* – the second person in the hierarchy of the Department of State of our time.

2.1 EUGENE SCHUYLER, A DIPLOMAT FRIEND TO ROMANIA

Eugene Schuyler 1840-1890

The personality of the first diplomatic agent of the United States of America remains inscribed in our history for the commitment with which he had completed his mission and has supported out country.

Eugene Schuyler was born on February 26, 1840 in Ithaca, the state of New York. He graduated from Yale College, where he studied literature, philosophy, and foreign languages. In 1859 he was awarded his PhD degree at the Yale University, and in 1863 he graduated legal studies at Columbia Law School. He was admitted in the diplomatic corps in 1866.

As he spoke very well Russian, he was appointed consul in the Russian Empire, to Moscow, a position he has held for several years. He met the writer Ivan Turgheniev (1818-1883) at Baden-Baden. He has developed and cherished close friendship relations with Lev Nikolaievici Tolstoi (1828-1910). Their friendship resulted in his translating into English the novel The Cossacks, as well as in his spending holidays at Iasnaia Poliana, Tolstoi's estate. Moreover, Schuyler translated several of Turgheniev's writings.

Casa Capşa, the residence of the first American ambassador to Bucharest

In 1870 he was appointed secretary of the American legation to Petersburg until 1876. During that period, he has worked on the English language edition of the national Finnish epic Kalevala and has written a book on Peter the Great, the Russian czar from 1682 until 1725. Schuyler also wrote travel memoirs about Russia and Central Asia of that time. He served as a consul general to Constantinople between 1876 and 1879, then he was appointed consul general to Rome in 1879, only to start his term to Bucharest on June 11, 1880.

His mission in Romania was a successful one, laying the bases on a steady and long-lasting relation, of more than one century. In 1880 he worked as Chargé d'Affaires in Romania, then he was a resident minister from 1880-1882, and starting from January 1883 he moved from Athens to Bucharest and he lived at Casa Capşa. The headquarters of the American legation was at 9 Puţul de Piatră Street, while the headquarters of the consulate was at 162 Calea Victoriei. It's worth mentioning that back then, just as at the present, there were cases when diplomatic representatives were endorsed for several states. Schuyler was acknowledged for Romania, Serbia, and Greece.

Eugene Schuyler boosted the commercial and cultural links between Romania and the United States of America. On April 11, 1881 Eugene Schuyler clenched with the Romanian authorities a *trade and navigation agreement* while providing "the most favoured nation" clause to our country. The merchandise import was thus stimulated, and our country imported machinery for agriculture, cotton, vegetal oils, textiles, and shoes. We must emphasize that the trade balance was in favour of the United States for economic reasons, as well as for their actual power to support trade at international level. Romania used to export leather, food, and some oil products. Many historians consider that the United States and Romania have had a powerful commercial relation in the field of oil products and machine tool. We consider that each state imported whichever it deemed necessary to meet its own economic needs, just as it has been the case throughout history. Eugene Schuyler and Vasile Boerescu concluded the first *Romanian-American consular agreement* on June 17, 1881.

Called back to his office in Bucharest, Schuyler resumed his academic career, to teach at the Cornell and John Hopkins Universities, while accomplishing a last diplomatic career, the one of consul general of the United States to Cairo, Egypt, where he fell ill with malaria and died on July 16, 1890 in Venice, where he was buried in the San Michele cemetery.

Eugene Schuyler was an active diplomat and he has extensively strengthened the Romanian-American relations, being a model for his successors, whom we shall briefly mention below. Schuyler was an important supporter of the establishment of a modern diplomatic service of the United States, being a precursor or Rogers Act (1924), which is known as the *Foreign Service Act*. Rogers Act is a package of legal norms regulating the way the diplomatic and consular services of the United States of America should be run. The designation of the act comes from John Jacob Rogers (1881-1925), a member of the House of Representatives in the Congress of the United States of America from 1913 until 1925, known as the father of such legislation.

Eugene Schuyler's personality has been decisive for the fate of the Romanian–American relations. We shall now list the representatives of the United States of America to Romania, while *emphasizing that one single diplomat has served twice in office to Bucharest, whereas two diplomats have failed to take their office,* until the Great Unification of 1918. The dates mentioned below are the nomination date and the year when each diplomat was called back in office. We need to remind that there is a deadline for taking one's diplomatic office which is related to each country's laws, and to other political and diplomatic events.

1. Eugene Schuyler (1840-189): December 14, 1880 – September 17, 1884
2. Walker Frean (1832-1899): April 18, 1885 – October 24, 1889
3. Archibald Loudon Snowden (1856-1932): July 1, 1889 – August 18, 1892
4. Eben Alexander (1851-1910): April 7, 1893 – August 1, 1894, holding the rank of minister plenipotentiary. From that point on, all the representatives shall hold the rank of officers plenipotentiaries.
5. William Woodville Rockhill (1854-1914): July 8, 1897 – April 2, 1899, prior to his appointment he had been assistant of the Secretary of State Richard Olney (1835-1917, in office 1895-1897) from 1896 until 1897. He was the first diplomat to hold the highest position in the Department of State sent to Romania.
6. Arthur Sherburne Hardy (1847-1930): April 18, 1899 – March 13, 1901
7. Charles Spencer Francis (1853 - 1911): December 20, 1901 – December 24, 1902. On October 13, 1902, Henry L. Wilson was nominated and appointed ambassador to Romania but he refused the nomination and was sent as an ambassador to Mexico.
8. John Brinkerhoff Jackons (1862-1920): October 13, 1902 – July 15, 1905. **He has been the only**

American ambassador in the history to have hold two terms to Bucharest, at a few years' distance.

9. John Wallace Riddle Jr. (1864-1941): March 8, 1905 – January 23, 1907

10. Horace Greeley Knowles (1863-1937) : January 16, 1907 – February 4, 1909

11. Huntigton Wilson was nominated as a minister plenipotentiary on December 17, 1908. He took the oath, but has never accomplished his mission because on March 5, 1909 he was appointed assistant of the Secretaries of State Philander C. Knox (1853-1921) and William Jennings Bryan (1860-1925) until 1913. Prior to being nominated, he had been assistant of the Secretary of State Elihu Root (1845-1937) from 1906 until 1908. He was the second great federal servant sent as an ambassador to Romania. Quite a proof of appreciation and cooperation between the two states during that time.

12. Spencer Fayette Eddy (1873-1939): January 12, 1909 – September 29, 1909.

13. John Ridgley Carter (1864-1944): September 25, 1901 – October 24, 1911

14. John Brinkerhoff Jackons (1862-1920) had his second term from August 12, 1911 until October 28, 1913

15. Charles Joseph Vopicka (born Karel Josef Vopicka) lived from 1857 until 1935 and had one of the longest terms as ambassador in the history of the Romanian-American relations: 6 years and 10 months less a day, September 11, 1913 – July 10, 1920. He was a close friend of Queen Mary and he facilitated her trip to the Unites States of America,

as well as her receipt to Chicago in 1926.

Queen Mary at the balcony of the legation in Washington D.C. – picture taken from the website of the Romanian Embassy to the United States of America

These ambassadors strengthened the Romanian-American relations and allowed the United States' support during the First World War from 1917 until 1918, times during which, to quote Ion Stanciu, we were allies without an alliance; the historian was referring to the 1914-1920 period, to be more precise. This has been a close cooperation throughout time, the bilateral relations being only disrupted due to historical developments. We consider we have been *allied in order to develop an alliance,* a fact unfortunately accomplished only later, because of the mysterious ways of the History. Or else we can state our countries have been partners without a Partnership.

2.2 THE HELP PROVIDED BY THE UNITED STATES OF AMERICA DURING THE FIRST WORLD WAR, AS WELL AS FOR ACCOMPLISHING THE GREAT UNIFICATION

Once the diplomatic relations have become institutionalized and permanent, the evolution of the two states was shaken by the outbreak of the First World War. During those moments, one could notice to what extent the Romanian and the American peoples were friends and close to each other.

Prior to the war, the US president William Howard Taft (1857-1930, in office from 1909 until 1913) signed an executive order according to which the Romanian imports to the United States of America were subject to "the most favoured nation" clause. On April 17, 1912, an act initiated by the Romanian government and endorsed by the Parliament was placing the imports from the United States of America to Romania subject to the same clause, except for the import of oil products. 41 agreements were concluded from 1864 until 1917 to regulate the diplomatic, commercial, and political relations between Romania and the United States of America. Those agreements have also tackled the issue of oil products, knowing the increasing importance of the Romanian-American Oil Company incorporated in 1904 by Standard Oil, the large American company owned by John Davison Rockfeller (1839-1937) with his brother William Avery Rockfeller Jr. (1841-1922).

The outbreak of the First World War was a ferment to the national conscience, a hope for accomplishing a dream – the unification of the three Romanian countries – a dream come true on December 1st, 1918. The United States of America entered the war in April 1917, a move which changed the fate of the war.

The United States sent an American military mission to support Romania. The American president Thomas Woodrow Wilson (1856-1924, US President in office from 1913 until 1921) signed the documents providing a loan by 4 USD 20-million instalments to Romania. The issue risen was the lack of a Romanian representative to Washington D.C. to jointly acknowledge and certify those documents. The Royal Decree number 1027 of September 24, 1917 ruled to establish in the United States of America, in Washington D.C., the *first permanent Romanian office in the United States of America* having Dr. Constantin Angelescu (1869-1948) as head of the legation holding a rank of a minister plenipotentiary. The game of history made the latter take his office on the very day of January 15, 1918, the birth date of the great Romanian poet Mihai Eminescu. The Secretary of the legation was Prince Anton (Antoine) Bibescu (1878-1951), the future ambassador of Romania to the United States of America from 1921 until 1926.

Until the legation actually became operational, the American Red Cross got very actively involved and has tremendously helped the population in sheer suffering in Moldova, suffering caused by the war, by the lack of clothes, food, medicines, because of the houses destroyed, and other urgent needs for survival. The American Red Cross spent funds obtained from donations worth USD 1.5 million, it sent 6 wagons of sanitary and medical products, 30 wagons of textiles, shoes, and first necessity food. Because of the exanthematous typhus epidemics and of the lack of medical staff in Romania, the American Red Cross required the support of the US President Woodrow Wilson in November 1917. The president Wilson endorsed and authorized the Secretary of War Newton Diehl Baker Jr. (1871-1937, in office from 1916 until 1921) to send 100 military surgeons to Romania to help the Romanian military doctors. Unfortunately the American military surgeons did not arrive anymore because of the events in progress in Russia.

On December 21st, the American government paid the first USD 5 million instalment to Romania as a war support. The continuous support effort of the United States of America, our great friend, has also backed the ideal of our people. On November 6, 1918 the American government chaired by the President issued a release reading as follows: *The Government of the United States of America is deeply sympathetic to the spirit of unification and to the aspirations of the Romanians worldwide, and it shall not neglect to use its influence at the right time so that the fait political and territorial rights of the Romanian nation can be acquired and preserved against any foreign invasion.* We obtained this release through the work of the diplomat Vasile Stoica (1889-1959), an acquaintance of the great politician Ion C. (Ionel) Brătianu (1864- 1927), called ***In America for the Romanian matter.***

We can thus notice the extremely important support of the state to become the largest power at the end of the War.

AS A CONCLUSION – LOOKING TOWARDS THE FUTURE

After the war came to an end, the Romanian-American relations have gotten stronger, while the exchanges have occurred at several levels. We care to mention that the American people came to learn about the Romanian arts and culture through Enescu's music, Brâncuși's sculptures, through painting, but also due to translations of literature. Just like the Romanians could read translations from writers such as Edgar Allan Poe (1809-1849), John Griffith London, known as Jack London (1876-1916), Samuel Langhorne Clemens, aka Mark Twain (1835-1910), Walt Whitman (1819-1892), Lyman Frank Baum (1856-1919), and many others.

Once the diplomatic mission of the Doctor Constantin Angelescu completed, the secretary of the legation, Prince Anton (Antoine) Bibescu was appointed as an ambassador, his term lasting from February 25, 1921 until April 9, 1926. His name is relate to the purchase of the current building of the

Romanian Embassy to the United States of America, located at the crossroads of Sheridan Circle and of 23 Street in Washington D.C.; this headquarters was bought in 1921.

The headquarters of the Romanian Embassy at the crossroads of Sheridan Circle and 23 Street in Washington D.C.

On the background of the Romanian-American relations, we must state that the diplomat Peter Augustus Jay (1877-1933) was the first minister plenipotentiary exclusively in charge with Romania, as he served as an ambassador from June 30, 1921 until May 9, 1925.

Strengthening the bilateral relations also laid the bases for a deeper cooperation, which caused the Romanian-American relations to evolve in a steady context. Unfortunately, certain historic periods disrupted the course of these relations. The Romanian ambassador to the United States of America, Radu Irimescu (1890-1975) was reappointed in 1940, after King Charles the IInd abdicated on October 15, 1940. Because of the turmoil of the historical events, the diplomatic events were disrupted on December 12, 1941 and resumed on February 7, 1946 as a legation.

The headquarters of the US Embassy to Bucharest from 1941 until 2011

An important step was taken in 1964, on June 1st, when the American government upgraded the legation of the United States of America as an embassy, while William Avery Crawford (1915-2001) was appointed ambassador extraordinary and plenipotentiary of the United States of America to Romania with his residence in Bucharest from December 24, 1964 until October 10, 1965. Crawford was a minister plenipotentiary of the United States of America to Romania from November 28, 1961 until December 24, 1964.

As a proof that the bilateral relations came to a

higher level, the Chairman of the State Council Gheorghe Gheorghiu Dej signed the decree no. 233 on June 4, 1964, ruling that the Romanian legation to Washington was upgraded as an embassy, and the decree no. 409 of July 1964 to appoint the economist Petre Bălăceanu as an ambassador extraordinary and plenipotentiary of Romania to the United States of America with his residence in Washington D.C.

The Romanian-American relations have started around 170 years ago and they got institutional and perennial 140 years ago. Their evolution was related to History and to its course, yet we can conclude at the end of this early historical journey that back in that time our nations were **Partners without a Partnership.**

The current headquarters of the US Embassy to Bucharest – image taken from www.wikimapia.org